THE LITTLE BOOK OF ADVICE FOR FLOWER GARDENERS

First published in Great Britain in 2026 by Hamlyn, an imprint of Octopus Publishing Group Ltd
Carmelite House
50 Victoria Embankment
London EC4Y 0DZ
www.octopusbooks.co.uk

An Hachette UK Company
www.hachette.co.uk

The authorized representative in the EEA is Hachette Ireland, 8 Castlecourt Centre, Dublin 15, D15 XTP3, Ireland (email: info@hbgi.ie)

This material was previously published in *Ask: The 1000 Most-Asked Questions about Gardening*

Distributed in the US by
Hachette Book Group
1290 Avenue of the Americas,
4th and 5th Floors
New York, NY 10104

Distributed in Canada by
Canadian Manda Group
664 Annette St., Toronto,
Ontario, Canada M6S 2C8

ISBN: 978-0-60064-024-0
eISBN: 978-0-60064-025-7

A CIP catalogue record for this book is available from the British Library.

Printed and bound in China.

10 9 8 7 6 5 4 3 2 1

Publisher: Lucy Pessell
Designers: Isobel Platt & Alicia House
Editor: Katie Button
Assistant Editor: Samina Rahman
Production Managers:
Lucy Carter & Nic Jones

THE LITTLE BOOK OF ADVICE FOR FLOWER GARDENERS

DAPHNE LEDWARD

CONTENTS

INTRODUCTION

In the world of gardening, the same questions arise time and time again: how can I ensure my flowers bloom beautifully and often? What and when should I plant to get the best results? How should I make the most of my garden or outside space?

Drawing on years of experience in gardening, answering thousands of your questions as a panelist and researcher on shows such as BBC's *Gardeners' Question Time*, this book is the distillation of a lifetime of helping flower gardeners to create beautiful gardens that bring them joy.

Structured by season, and packed full of tips and easy-to-follow advice, find the answers to all of your flower gardening questions, all year round.

Good luck, and good gardening.

SPRING

"What is naturalizing?"

This is when you plant bulbs permanently to come up in the same place, such as under trees or in lawns, every year.

"Is there anything I should bear in mind when naturalizing bulbs in grass?"

Make sure you plant to the correct depth for each bulb. Never cut off the foliage before it starts to turn yellow. Choose a slow-growing grass mix that will not choke the bulbs.

"WHAT PLANTS CAN I GROW IN MY NATURAL GARDEN?"

Most daffodils, tulips, bluebells, crocuses, snowdrops (*Galanthus*) and fritillaries can be naturalized in grass.

"I FORGOT TO PLANT ANY SPRING BULBS LAST AUTUMN. WHAT SHOULD I DO?"

Most garden suppliers and many supermarkets sell them in pots in spring ready for planting. They are more expensive, but will give you an instant show.

"I've seen spring bulbs being sold off cheaply in midwinter. Are these a good buy?"

Yes. They will grow perfectly well, but the flowers may be a little later than normal.

"Can I plant hyacinths in the garden after they have been indoors?"

Yes, but the flowers will be smaller in subsequent years.

"What is meant by planting in the green?"

Some spring bulbs, such as snowdrops (*Galanthus*) and aconites, may take a while to start flowering again if you plant them as dry bulbs, so they should be dug up immediately after flowering but with the leaves still growing, then divided and replanted.

"WHAT HAPPENS IF YOU FORGET TO PLANT NARCISSI BULBS UNTIL THE SPRING?"

They will still flower, but they'll produce fewer leaves. The following year, most bulbs will be blind (produce no flowers), but afterwards they should flower as normal.

"Why have none of my daffodil bulbs flowered this year?"

They may need feeding, or they could be short of water. Make sure you water them during a dry spring. Overcrowded bulbs will also stop flowering: dig them up and replant after flowering or in early autumn.

"WHAT DO I DO WITH THE LEAVES OF SPRING BULBS AFTER FLOWERING?"

Leave them for at least six weeks before cutting them off, as they feed the bulbs. Do not tie them up or loop them in elastic bands.

"SHOULD I FEED MY DAFFODILS?"

Yes. After flowering, give them one or two applications of a balanced fertilizer or fish, blood and bone before the leaves die down.

“Are there any spring bulbs that will flower in dry shade under trees?”

Grape hyacinths (*Muscari*) will flower almost anywhere. Naturalize them in big clumps for the best effect. Eventually, they will spread by seed as well as offsets.

“Tall spring bulbs look out of place in my tiny garden. What can I plant instead?”

Try snowdrops (*Galanthus*), chionodoxa, dwarf narcissi, such as 'Tête-à-tête', botanical tulips, such as 'Red Riding Hood', crocuses, scillas and *Allium moly*.

"HOW LONG DO WINTER-FLOWERING PANSIES LAST?"

If they are in a position out of direct hot sun, and if you deadhead them regularly and remember to feed and water them, they could last nearly all summer.

"CAN I SAVE SPRING BEDDING PLANTS FROM YEAR TO YEAR?"

Daisies (*Bellis*), pansies, sweet Williams (*Dianthus barbatus*), wallflowers (*Erysimum*) and some forget-me-nots (*Myosotis*) are short-lived perennials, and will last for a second year, but the flowering is always best the first year, so it is not worth it. Primulas and polyanthus can be divided to make more plants after flowering, and will last for many seasons.

“Is it worth saving the seedling forget-me-nots that come up in the garden?”

Generally, these will be a motley lot, but in an informal setting *Myosotis* seedlings can be allowed to grow up between other plants for an early flush.

“When should I sow wallflowers for next spring?”

Sow any time from late spring until early summer.

“I BOUGHT SOME CANTERBURY BELLS FOR MY HERBACEOUS BORDER. WHY DID THEY DIE AFTER FLOWERING?”

This plant (*Campanula medium*) is a true biennial – that is, it grows one year and flowers, seeds and dies the next, so this was to be expected.

"WHAT DO I LOOK FOR IN A GOOD BEDDING PLANT?"

Choose bushy specimens with healthy-looking leaves. Avoid those in full flower and with many roots coming out of the container base.

"I have an unheated greenhouse but want to grow my own bedding plants. How can I get a head start with my planting?"

Buy plug plants from seed companies and young plant specialists. These are usually dispatched for growing on when no extra heat is needed in the greenhouse.

"WHEN IS THE RIGHT TIME TO PLANT OUT SUMMER BEDDING PLANTS?"

Wait until all risk of frost has passed, usually late spring. Retail outlets often sell bedding plants ready for planting out far too early.

"What is the cheapest way of getting a quick, showy display in summer?"

Use hardy annuals. Sown in mid-spring, they will be in flower by midsummer. Most will produce a second flush if deadheaded after flowering.

"WHAT IS A HARDY ANNUAL?"

This is a plant that germinates, grows, flowers, seeds and dies in one season, and that can be sown outdoors in spring.

"Is there any way I can grow bedding plants without a greenhouse or cold frame?"

Some bedding plants, such as tobacco plants (*Nicotiana*) and French and African marigolds (*Tagetes*) can be sown outdoors in situ in early summer to give a good display in late summer and autumn.

"What is carpet bedding?"

This is a bedding scheme consisting of low-growing plants, often succulents or plants with interesting foliage, in a complex pattern. It can be used to good effect in front or small gardens, but watch out as they require a lot of attention.

"IS IT WORTH BUYING END-OF-SEASON BEDDING PLANTS?"

If they are stunted and root-bound, it is unlikely they will make good plants; otherwise, if you want to fill up some gaps, they are worth a try.

"CAN I SAVE MY OWN SEED FROM BEDDING PLANTS?"

Many will not come true to their parents, but it is always interesting to see what comes up.

"What should I use to feed bedding plants?"

A weekly feed with a high-potash liquid fertilizer (such as tomato feed) may be necessary for containerized bedding plants; in good soil, they require little extra feeding.

"I want to grow some annuals on a trellis as a temporary screen. What would do best?"

Sweet peas (*Lathyrus odoratus*) are the obvious choice, but you could also try trailing nasturtiums, morning glory (*Ipomoea tricolor*) or black-eyed Susans (*Thunbergia*).

"Is spring too late to prune?"

If the new shoots are long, it is better just to remove dead and dying wood and prune harder from late autumn to early spring next time.

"WHEN SHOULD I FEED MY ROSES?"

Feed with a specific rose fertilizer in early spring, and again after the first flush of flowers in early to midsummer.

"How long can I expect a rose bush to live?"

This depends on the cultivar and how well it is looked after, but a period in excess of 30 years is not unusual.

"CAN YOU RECOMMEND SOME FOOLPROOF BUSH ROSES?"

The hybrid tea roses 'Silver Jubilee' (pink), and 'Royal William' (crimson), and the floribunda roses 'Sweet Dream' (apricot) and 'Iced Ginger' (ivory/copper pink) are healthy growers with excellent disease resistance.

"What is the difference between hybrid tea and floribunda roses?"

Floribunda roses have heads with many flowers; hybrid teas have a single flower or just a few blooms on each stem.

"What is the difference between a climbing rose and a rambler?"

A rambler usually flowers only once in a season, then produces the flowering wood for the following year. A climbing rose flowers on wood produced in the current season.

"My climbing roses flower at the top of their trellises. How can I make them flower lower down?"

Untie them completely, pull down all the stems until they are as close to horizontal as possible, then re-tie. Shorter, flowering shoots will soon form along the stems.

"I have many established shrub roses that have become rather untidy. How can I tidy them up?"

Shrub roses can last for many years without regular pruning, but when they start to get out of hand, cut them back hard into the old wood between late autumn and early spring and feed well.

"I HAVE NO BARE EARTH, BUT I WANT TO GROW A CLIMBING ROSE. CAN I PLANT ONE IN A CONTAINER?"

You need as big a container as you can manage and good-quality soil-based compost. Top-dress each spring and apply a good rose fertilizer; keep well watered, and give a liquid feed every week during the growing season.

"Can I underplant my roses with ground-cover plants?"

It is possible, but these plants will compete with the roses for food and water, so you may find the roses do not thrive as well.

"Do ground-cover roses help with controlling weeds?"

Ground-cover roses are really only roses with a lax habit that makes them suitable for training over the soil. Weeds can still find their way through the shoots.

"THE LEAVES OF MY ROSES HAVE DEEP BITES ROUND THE EDGES. WHAT HAS CAUSED THIS?"

This damage is caused by the leaf-cutter bee. It will not harm your plants, so there is no need to take action.

"I have a lot of naturalized bulbs in my lawn. When can I start mowing?"

You will have to wait until six weeks after the flowers have died. The area will look rather pale and rough after the first cut, but will soon recover and blend in.

"I planted a lot of spring bulbs last autumn but none have come up. Why?"

Mice or squirrels might have eaten the bulbs. Try covering the soil surface with plastic netting, pegged down at the sides.

"IS IT POSSIBLE TO HAVE A CHAMOMILE LAWN?"

Lawn chamomile (*Chamaemelum nobile*) takes a long time to establish and must be weeded regularly until the plants knit together. The plants are comparatively expensive and not as hard-wearing as grass. Try a small area first to see how you get on.

"HOW CAN I GET RID OF A LOW, CLOVER-LIKE PLANT WITH YELLOW FLOWERS THAT IS GROWING IN MY LAWN? IT DOES NOT RESPOND TO WEEDKILLERS."

This is yellow suckling clover or lesser yellow trefoil (*Trifolium dubium*). It spreads by seeds and runners, so pull up or dig out as much as possible. Lower the mower blades to remove the flowerheads and repeat weedkiller treatments regularly.

“WHAT COMPOST OR SOIL SHOULD I USE TO FILL RAISED BEDS?”

Large raised beds can be filled with good topsoil with some well-rotted manure or garden compost added. Smaller beds are best filled with soil-based compost.

“What are the optimum dimensions for a raised bed?”

Your beds should be no more than 1.2 m (4 ft) wide and 3 m (about 10 ft) long, so that you have good access to the soil from different sides.

“A friend has used railway sleepers to make his raised beds. Is this wise?”

It is said that some of the wood preservative will leach out of the timber and damage the crops, but usually the sleepers have weathered sufficiently for this not to be a problem.

"What should I use for the walls of my raised beds?"

Twin-wall, recycled PVC boards are available online and from some seed companies. They take up little space, have good insulating properties and can be moved easily if necessary.

"I WOULD LIKE TO PUT SOME RAISED BEDS ON MY PATIO. CAN I PUT THEM DIRECTLY ON THE SLABS?"

You may find that if they are there for more than one season they will stain the slabs, so cover the slabs with polythene first. You also need to check that the water can drain away properly.

"WHY DO I HAVE TO PRUNE?"

It depends on the type of plant. Roses are pruned to encourage flower production, shrubs to keep them young and healthy, trees for shape, and so on.

"Do I have to prune shrubs every year?"

No. Young specimens may need pruning annually at first to encourage strong growth; after that, pruning is usually done when the branches get overcrowded or no new wood is produced.

"What happens if you cut an old rose bush back really hard?"

If it is healthy, it might produce new shoots. Otherwise, it probably won't recover. If you are fond of it, treat it gently.

"WHEN DO I PRUNE A HYDRANGEA?"

Never, if you can help it. To keep it a reasonable size, remove about one-third of the old shoots at ground level in spring every year to produce new shoots from the base. In this way, you will always have flowers, plus young wood that will flower the following year, and the whole bush will be rejuvenated in four years. If you cut back all the shoots, you will remove the flowering wood as well. However, if the plant is overgrown, you may find it better to cut it back to ground level and sacrifice the flowers for one season.

"When is the best time to prune a magnolia?"

Never! If you need to prune a magnolia you have chosen the wrong type. Cutting off shoots will make matters worse and affect flowering. Instead, remove the lower branches completely so you open up the space beneath.

“My English lavender bush has got leggy. How can I improve it?”

You must remember to trim lavender regularly. It should be pruned every year after flowering by removing most of the current season’s soft shoots, but it will not regrow from woody branches.

“I have a hedge of laurustinus (*Viburnum tinus*), which I trim in autumn every year. Why does it never produce flowers?”

You are trimming off all the flowering shoots. In future, trim in spring.

“WHEN SHOULD I PRUNE A ROSEMARY BUSH?”

The best time is in late spring or early summer, so it has a chance to recover before the frosts.

"MY FORSYTHIA IS BEAUTIFUL EVERY YEAR. I NEVER PRUNE IT. SHOULD I?"

It's not essential, but if you remove a few old branches after flowering every year, the bush will live longer.

"When should I trim winter-flowering heathers?"

Clip after flowering every spring, but do not cut back too hard or they will not recover.

"I have a bougainvillea in my conservatory that is getting out-of-hand. Can I prune it?"

Shorten all the shoots back to the supports. It will start producing bracts on new wood later in the season.

“What’s wrong with my hebes? They look sick and some have died.”

They have probably been affected by the fungal disease mildew. Trim the live shoots back lightly and spray immediately with a fungicide. You may need to repeat this at two- to three-week intervals throughout the summer.

"My Pyracantha (firethorn) is covered in white fluff. What is it?"

This is woolly aphid, which is difficult to deal with, as it is waterproof and cannot be contained with contact insecticides. A systemic insecticide will kill woolly aphid temporarily, but washing it off with a strong jet of water is just as effective and lasts just as long.

“MY JUDAS TREE IS DYING BACK. THE DEAD WOOD HAS ORANGE SPOTS ON IT.”

This is coral spot, a fungal disease. It mainly affects dead branches, but in some shrubs, like *Cercis siliquastrum*, it can spread into live wood and kill it. Remove all affected parts completely as soon as you see them.

“WHAT HAS CAUSED THE LITTLE, TORTOISE-LIKE SWELLINGS ALL OVER THE BRANCHES OF MY OLEANDER?”

Scale insects affect many outdoor and conservatory plants. Where the affected plant is growing in a pot, watering with a vine weevil killer will control it for three months or more. The remains can be removed with an old toothbrush.

SUMMER

"What is meant by half-hardy on the labels of some plants?"

This is the term used to describe plants that will grow happily outdoors during the summer, but cannot tolerate frost and will need the protection of a slightly heated greenhouse in winter. Many patio plants, like Brugmansia, lantana and citrus, fall into this category.

"I cannot keep my perennial wallflowers alive for more than a year or two. Where am I going wrong?"

They are naturally short-lived plants, but are easily propagated from cuttings in summer.

"WHAT SHOULD I DO WITH LUPINS AND DELPHINIUMS AFTER THEY HAVE FINISHED FLOWERING?"

Cut them down almost to soil level. They may produce a second flower flush later in the season.

"My flower border is dry. Are there any perennials that will do well here?"

First, dig in plenty of organic material to help hold water. *Achillea*, *Echinops* (globe thistle), *Kniphofia* (red hot poker), nerines and *Stachys* are just a few perennials that should thrive in these conditions.

"MY GARDEN IS IN PERMANENT SHADE FROM THE HOUSE NEXT DOOR. ARE PERENNIALS OUT OF THE QUESTION?"

No. Try *Alchemilla mollis, Darmera peltata, Caltha, Trollius* and hostas for an attractive effect.

"Some nurseries recommend hostas for dry situations, some for moist. Which is correct?"

Hostas are, in fact, pretty tough and will withstand a wide range of conditions.

"How can I stop my flower border always looking a mess because the plants flop over?"

Provide supports before the plants have grown too tall. They will never look right if they are tied up after they have flopped.

"I bought a pampas grass *(Cortaderia)* five years ago and it has never flowered. I have been told this is because I do not set fire to it every spring. Is this true?"

This is often recommended as a way of both tidying it up and giving it a dose of potash to help it flower at the same time, but it can also set fire to the roots, so cutting back is better. It sounds as if yours is a poor seedling plant. Dig it up and replace it in late summer with one already showing plumes.

"I had some beautiful Himalayan poppies *(Meconopsis)*, but this year they have disappeared."

Many of them die after flowering. Do not deadhead and you are likely to get seedlings the following year.

"CAN YOU SUGGEST A PERENNIAL TO EDGE A ROSE BORDER?"

Catmint (*Nepeta*) is often used for this. Cut it back regularly in summer to keep the plants neat and to encourage flowering.

"I HAVE A SUNNY, MOIST PATCH AT THE BOTTOM OF MY GARDEN. WHAT HARDY PERENNIALS SHOULD I PLANT THERE?"

There are plenty that like these conditions. Try *Ligularia, Caltha, Filipendula, Euphorbia palustris, Omphalodes, Lythrum, Rodgersia* and *Lysimachia*.

"Can hardy perennials be mixed with other kinds of plants?"

Definitely. They can really brighten up a shrubbery or add interest to a rose bed.

"I'm gardening on a budget and can't afford to pay the prices most garden stores charge for hardy perennials. Is there an alternative?"

If you don't mind waiting, most of the common kinds are easily raised from seed, and some will even flower in their first season. Check the seed brochures for what is available.

"COULD I MAKE A PERENNIAL BED IN THE MIDDLE OF MY LAWN?"

Yes, but remember that the bed will be seen from all sides, so put the tall perennials in the middle, not at the back. Choose sturdy, shorter-growing varieties.

"How can I get rid of the bindweed growing through my herbaceous border?"

Wait until the bindweed (*Convolvulus*) has grown to about 30 cm (12 in) high, then paint the leaves with glyphosate. Several applications may be necessary.

"I HAVE A NEW HERBACEOUS BORDER AND IT LOOKS SPARSE. HAVE I SPACED THE PLANTS OUT TOO MUCH?"

No, they need room to establish. Fill in with annuals and summer bulbs for temporary interest.

"SHOULD I MULCH AN HERBACEOUS BORDER?"

Mulching in late spring or early summer will conserve moisture and deter weeds.

"SHOULD I CUT MY PERENNIALS BACK AT THE END OF SUMMER?"

Most gardeners like to tidy the borders at the end of the season, but slightly tender perennials, like *Kniphofia* and penstemons, are best left till spring.

"What is the purpose of deadheading?"

It is done to encourage the plant to put all its energy into producing new flowering shoots for a second flush.

"What is the correct technique when deadheading?"

Strictly speaking, you should remove both the spent flowerhead and the stem below to the first leaf with five leaflets. In practice, the results are just as good if you just pinch out the dead flower.

“CAN YOU SUGGEST SOME CLIMBING ROSES TO GROW UP OBELISKS?”

Choose moderate-growing varieties with an upright habit, such as 'Aloha', 'Golden Showers', 'Joseph's Coat' and 'Handel'.

"Is there a chemical-free way of preventing disease in roses?"

Choose new cultivars that have been bred for disease resistance. Space them well apart, keep the soil moist and feed them at least twice a season.

"WHAT IS MEANT BY ENGLISH ROSES?"

This group has flowers that resemble the old shrub roses, but they are repeat flowering and can be formally pruned as floribundas or lightly tidied like old-fashioned shrub roses.

“Can I use grass clippings as a mulch on a rose bed?”

Yes. The mulch will keep the roots cool and moist, but if you have annual meadow grass in your lawn, you may get problems with seedlings from this practice.

“I planted some ground-cover roses in a narrow bed between my house and the drive, and they are spreading too far. How can I control them?”

Treat them as climbers. Put training wires or trellis on the wall and train them up this. They can be pruned as ramblers, or just clipped over lightly after flowering and again in spring.

“WHEN AND HOW SHOULD I PRUNE A ROSE HEDGE?”

Prune after the first flush of flowers and again in autumn – unless the roses bear ornamental hips, in which case you should prune in winter or early spring.

“I WOULD LIKE TO GROW ROSES WITH HIPS THAT I CAN MAKE INTO WINE.”

The best for this is any cultivar of *Rosa rugosa*. Even if you are not a wine-maker, the hips will extend the season of interest.

“I have a ‘Dorothy Perkins’ rambler trained as a weeping standard. How and when should I prune it?”

Prune immediately after flowering by removing all the flowered stems. Tie in the new growths as soon as they are long enough.

"Are containerized roses worth the extra money?"

They will enable you to plant during the growing season, but need extra care while they establish.

"I intend to buy some new roses in the autumn. Is there anything I should be doing now?"

The best and most enjoyable job is to visit rose fields and public gardens to get an idea of what you want and how they perform.

"WHAT ARE PATIO ROSES?"

These are a type of short-growing, modern bush roses with a compact habit that makes them suitable for growing in beds near patios and paths and also in containers. Examples are 'Top Marks' and 'Sweet Dream'.

"IS IT POSSIBLE TO GROW MINIATURE ROSES IN WINDOW BOXES?"

Yes. Choose small cultivars, such as 'Pour Toi' and 'Estru', and use soil-based compost.

"THERE ARE SEED HEADS ON MANY OF MY ROSES. CAN I GROW NEW ONES FROM THESE?"

Yes, but they will be nothing like the parent. It will be years before you know what sort of plant you have produced, but it can be interesting to see the results.

"THE HEAD OF MY STANDARD ROSE HAS DIED. CAN I CUT THE STEM BACK AND START AGAIN?"

No. The stem is only a rootstock, and you will get wild-rose-type flowers from it.

"I have a large evergreen Ceanothus and would like to prune it back. When and how should I do this?"

Evergreen shrubs flowering until midsummer should be pruned after flowering; those flowering later in the year are best pruned in spring. Thin out overcrowded branches and cut back the rest to promote new growth.

"My clematis gets brown leaves all up the stems as the summer progresses. What is the matter with it?"

This is to be expected with most climbers, and no amount of pruning will ever fix the problem. Try planting a shrub in front of it if you feel it looks unsightly.

“WHEN DOES A CLIMBING HYDRANGEA START TO FLOWER?”

It can take several years for this climber to establish itself. Usually once it starts to climb, it will also start to produce flowers.

“I AM TOLD I SHOULD CUT MY FLOWERING ALMOND BACK HARD EVERY YEAR. WHEN SHOULD I DO THIS?”

Prunus triloba flowers on new wood produced after flowering in spring, so it should be cut back in early summer to keep it tidy.

“I have an established lilac hedge. When can I prune it so it flowers next summer?”

Prune lilac (*Syringa*) immediately after flowering, but do not cut back hard.

"When should I plant dahlia tubers?"

Plant them in late spring to early summer, after the risk of frost.

"My dahlia tubers are huge. Can I divide them?"

Yes. Dahlia tubers can be divided every other year to increase your stock.

"HOW DEEP SHOULD I PLANT DAHLIA TUBERS?"

Plant taller cultivars 8 cm (3 in) deep, and bedding and shorter types 5 cm (2 in) deep.

"HOW CAN I GROW A PINEAPPLE LILY *(EUCOMIS)*?"

Plant the bulb in a container and give it winter protection. Alternatively, grow it in a well-drained, warm, sunny border.

"I HAVE NO LUCK KEEPING BEGONIAS AFTER THE FIRST YEAR. WHAT SHOULD I BE DOING DIFFERENTLY?"

At the end of summer, once all the foliage has dropped off, remove them from their containers and discard the old compost (which may contain the eggs of vine weevil grubs). Store them in a single layer in a cool, dry, frost-free, dark place in sand or peat substitute until spring.

"I think I've planted my begonias upside down. Will they grow?"

Not well. The slightly convex part of the tuber should be at the top; the rounded side is the bottom.

"I have no luck growing lilies in the garden. What conditions do they like?"

Most species of lily prefer neutral or slightly acid, humus-rich soil. Modern hybrids can cope with a wider range of conditions, but in all cases, the soil must not be overwet.

"My soil does not suit lilies, but I love to see them appearing among other flowers in the herbaceous border. What can I do?"

Plant about six bulbs in a large pot. When the lilies are about to flower, put the pot in the border.

"HOW DO I GET A SUCCESSION OF GLADIOLI FLOWERS THROUGHOUT THE SUMMER?"

Plant the corms at fortnightly intervals through spring to early summer.

“I HAVE SEEN A PURPLE, GLADIOLUS-LIKE FLOWER IN A PARK. WHAT IS THIS?”

This is *Gladiolus communis* subsp. *byzantinus*. It is fairly hardy and will usually survive temperatures below freezing without lifting.

"How can I stop my gladioli from flopping over?"

The only way to prevent this is to stake each plant at the time the corm is planted.

"CAN I LEAVE A CANNA IN THE GROUND ALL THE YEAR ROUND?"

No. Cannas are half-hardy and must be lifted and dried off in autumn before being stored in a frost-free place.

"I bought a lot of cannas in pots last year, but many of them look poorly this summer. What is wrong with them?"

They may be suffering from a virus. There is no cure and you should discard diseased plants. If you are buying cannas in full leaf, reject any that have stunted, streaked or deformed leaves.

"WHY DO MY ARUM LILIES (*ZANTEDESCHIA AETHIOPICA*) NEVER FLOWER?"

The flowering shoots probably get damaged by frost. Grow them in pots in a cool greenhouse and put outdoors in late spring.

"ARE THERE ANY SUMMER BULBS I CAN STILL PLANT IN EARLY SUMMER?"

Tigridia, chincherinchee (*Ornithogalum thyrsoides*) and *Childanthus fragrans* can still be planted at this time.

"I BOUGHT SEVERAL EYE-CATCHING CALLA LILIES IN FLOWER AT A GARDEN SHOW TWO YEARS AGO. WHY HAVEN'T THEY FLOWERED SINCE THEN?"

Like *Zantedeschia aethiopica*, they need humus-rich, permanently moist soil, but are much more difficult to get into flower after the first year.

"I would love to grow freesias outdoors. Is this possible in a temperate climate?"

For reliable flowers, you will need to buy specially prepared corms. Plant them 5–8 cm (2–3 in) deep in late spring and early summer for late-summer flowers. They are tender plants, and you could grow them in containers, which should be kept in a frost-free place in winter.

"What is the tall, hyacinth-like plant that flowers in late summer?"

This is *Galtonia candicans*. You can plant the bulbs in spring or even early summer. They are hardy, and for best results you should leave the bulbs undisturbed once established.

"MY NEW HOUSE HAS A PAVED GARDEN, WHICH LOOKS BARE. CAN YOU SUGGEST SOME YEAR-ROUND INTEREST I CAN GROW IN POTS?"

Use large pots of soil-based compost and plant a nucleus of variegated forms of evergreen shrubs, such as hebes, *Euonymus fortunei*, osmanthus and holly (*Ilex*). All these can be pruned regularly to keep them in check. Underplant with spring bulbs and fill out with bedding plants.

“What is the best soluble fertilizer for a hanging basket?”

Tomato food or a specific container feed is most effective.

“HOW OFTEN SHOULD I WATER A HANGING BASKET?”

In normal summer weather, once a day may be enough, but in hot, sunny weather, they need watering two or three times a day.

“MY BASKETS SEEM TO LOOK TIRED EARLY IN THE SEASON. HOW CAN I KEEP THEM LOOKING GOOD FOR LONGER?”

Never forget to feed and water, and deadhead regularly to give a succession of flowers.

"THERE IS A CONCRETE PATH ALL AROUND MY HOUSE. CAN I GROW A CLEMATIS AGAINST THE HOUSE WALL?"

Clematis in containers need good-quality, soil-based compost, which must never be allowed to get even slightly dry. Feed with rose fertilizer in spring and summer.

"What is the best way to train jasmine and bougainvillea?"

After pruning, train the new shoots in a loop around a wire framework or trellis.

"All the leaves started to fall off my bougainvillea, and I found the pot was standing in water. Will it recover?"

More plants are killed by overwatering than underwatering. Allow the compost to dry out and the bougainvillea will usually recover.

"Why do my honeysuckle flowers die before they open?"

This is probably caused by mildew. Spray with a fungicide before the problem occurs, and be sure to keep the roots cool and moist.

"What has made the shoots of my honeysuckle distorted and sticky?"

Aphids are sucking the sap of the young growths. Spray with an insecticide immediately or flowering will be affected.

"SOME OF MY ROSE LEAVES HAVE BEEN SKELETONIZED. WHAT HAS CAUSED THIS?"

The rose slugworm has caused this damage. It can be curbed by an insecticide, but will not kill the plants, so is best left alone.

AUTUMN

"MY HERBACEOUS BORDER IS COMPLETELY OVERRUN WITH COUCH GRASS. IS THERE A CHEMICAL I CAN TREAT IT WITH?"

Any chemical that will kill couch grass will also kill the plants in the border. The best way to get rid of this weed is to lift the plants in autumn, split them and pick out every bit of couch grass root. Dig over the border and remove all the roots from the border soil before you replant your perennials.

"When should I split the perennials in my herbaceous border?"

The recommendation is every three years, but if they are doing well, there is no need to do this job until flowering and growth are affected. Autumn or early spring are the best times.

"I am making a rose bed. Is it better to mix cultivars or stick to the same kind?"

A hotchpotch of cultivars, especially if they have different habits, can look rather bitty. Choose one cultivar only with similar heights and habits.

"HOW LONG DO I HAVE TO CONTINUE SPRAYING ROSES AGAINST DISEASE?"

It depends on the weather. If the roses stop growing and flowering in autumn, you can stop then. However, in some mild autumns and winters, the roses never stop growing until pruned, in which case, a three- or four-weekly spray may still be necessary.

"My roses were badly affected by black spot this year and most of the leaves have now fallen off. Can I compost these?"

No. It is better not to because disease spores may be spread when you use the compost.

"My roses are flowering late this year. Will it spoil them if I do not cut them off?"

No. When you prune them, new flowering shoots will be produced.

"I WAS TIDYING MY RAMBLER ROSES AND FOUND LOTS OF NEW, LONG SHOOTS THAT IT SEEMS A SHAME TO CUT OFF. WHAT SHOULD I DO WITH THEM?"

See if you can replan your garden so that these shoots can be trained on chains or wires alongside the lawn or over a flowerbed.

"SHOULD I PUT ROSE FERTILIZER ON MY ROSE BED IN AUTUMN?"

Most rose feeds are quick-acting and will either keep the roses growing when they should be dormant or will be completely wasted. If you want to feed your roses, use coarse bone meal or granulated (not powdered) hoof and horn fertilizer.

"CAN YOU SUGGEST A ROSE FOR WINTER INTEREST? MOST ROSES LOOK SO DRAB."

Rosa sericea f. *pteracantha* has large, translucent red thorns. Autumn is a good time to plant it, as it will have a chance to make a good bush for the following autumn and winter.

"When a rose bush is planted, does the part of the plant where the branches come from go above or beneath the soil?"

This is where the rose cultivar was budded on to the rootstock, and it should be buried about 2.5 cm (1 in) below soil level. This is so the cultivar itself also makes roots, so when the bush is established, it will have a large, strong root system that will produce a healthy plant with many branches coming from near the base.

"I have just bought some bare-root rose bushes and nearly all the roots have been chopped off. Will the rose survive?"

This may have been for the convenience of the packer, but hard root pruning actually does no harm at all, as it encourages fibrous feeding roots to form.

"I BOUGHT SOME ROSES IN CONTAINERS FOR AUTUMN PLANTING. WHY DID THE COMPOST FALL OFF AS I WAS PUTTING THEM IN THE HOLES?"

They may have been recently lifted and potted up. It does not matter at this time of year if the compost falls off; if you were planting bare-root bushes, they would have no compost on them anyway.

"I BOUGHT SOME BARE-ROOT ROSES AT A SUPERMARKET. THE ROOTS WERE WRAPPED IN HESSIAN (BURLAP) AND ELASTIC BANDS, AND THE INSTRUCTIONS SAID TO LEAVE THESE ON. SHOULD I?"

At this time of year, it is better not to. The roots will have been restricted by the wrapping and elastic bands, and will never make a good root system unless they are released.

"Should I protect less hardy marginals over winter?"

The tops will start dying back as the weather gets colder, but the water will insulate less hardy marginal plants, like arum lilies and *Lobelia cardinalis.*

"My marginal plants are in crates and are becoming overcrowded. Can I split and replant them in the autumn?"

Growth slows as the water cools. This can cause root rot in newly planted aquatics, so it is best to wait until late spring.

"Should I water specimens immediately after planting at this time of year?"

If you are planting during a dry spell, you should give the area a good soaking after planting.

"Should I apply a mulch after planting in autumn?"

Mulching will keep warm soil at a higher temperature than normal for longer. As well as preventing moisture loss, it will help to establish the plants quicker.

"WHAT ARE COCOA SHELLS USED FOR?"

They can be used as a mulch or dug in as a soil improver before planting. As a mulch, the shells can become soggy during wet periods, so are best used around woody plants, like trees, shrubs, roses and fruit.

"IS IT TRUE YOU CAN GET CROCUSES THAT FLOWER IN AUTUMN?"

Crocus speciosus will flower from early autumn to midwinter according to cultivar. Plant corms in late summer in a sunny, well-drained spot.

"WHAT SHOULD I AVOID WHEN I'M BUYING BULBS FOR SPRING?"

Avoid outlets where the bulbs are kept in warm conditions, because this will encourage premature growth and the spread of disease. Also, do not buy soft bulbs or those with long shoots already growing.

"Should I peel the brown skin from tulip bulbs before replanting them?"

No. The skin is there to protect the bulbs from damage and disease. Unless the skin is loose and comes off when handling, it should be left alone.

“I have bought several sacks of daffodil bulbs for naturalizing in grass. Should I plant each bulb individually with a bulb planter?”

Although this technique is recommended, it is much too much like hard work. Peel back the turf about 5 cm (2 in) thick so you can plant the bulbs in groups, lightly fork over the soil underneath, position the bulbs on the surface about 8–10 cm (3–4 in) apart and replace the turf carefully. Firm gently: any slight bumps will disappear as the bulbs start to grow.

"Some of my narcissus bulbs appear to be two bulbs joined together. Should I separate these before planting?"

You can separate them if they are the same size, but they will make a better show if left together. Large bulbs with small offsets should be planted intact; the offsets will not flower until they reach a certain size.

“I ACCIDENTALLY DUG UP SOME NARCISSUS BULBS WHEN I WAS CLEARING A BORDER. THEY HAD STARTED TO SHOOT. I REPLANTED THEM IMMEDIATELY. WAS THIS THE RIGHT THING TO DO?”

Yes. If this happens, try not to damage either the roots or the shoots, and do not be tempted to split the clumps by pulling them apart. Discard bulbs that have been cut in half.

"WHAT IS THE DIFFERENCE BETWEEN SPECIES AND HYBRID OR DUTCH CROCUSES? I'VE SEEN BOTH TYPES OF CORM FOR SALE."

Species crocuses are those that either grow naturally in the wild or have been bred closely from them. They generally flower early. Large-flowered hybrids flower later and have bigger flowers. To get a show for as long as possible in spring, you need to have a selection of both.

“The crocuses in my mixed border are getting very overcrowded. When should I dig them up and split them?”

Autumn is the best time if you can find the dormant clumps, otherwise do it in early summer, just after the leaves have shrivelled.

"A friend has offered to give me some spring-flowering bulbs from her garden. Should I accept them?"

Find out if they are healthy and have been flowering well. If you do not know, it is better not to introduce them into your garden.

"I SEE ON THE LABELS OF MANY BULB PACKETS THAT MOST BULBS ARE OFFERED FOR SALE FROM CULTIVATED STOCK. WHY IS THIS IMPORTANT?"

In some parts of the world, wild bulb stocks have been almost completely destroyed by being dug up and sold on for garden cultivation. In Britain, it is illegal to dig up wild bulbs, like bluebells, and replant or sell them on.

"Should I water my spring bulbs once I have planted them?"

This will not be necessary from autumn to spring, although watering after the flowers have faded will encourage better flowering the following year.

“I LOVE THE TALL, LARGE-FLOWERED TULIPS, BUT IN MY GARDEN THEY FALL OVER, AND THIS PUTS ME OFF PLANTING THEM. WHAT CAN I DO?”

Provide them with stakes at planting time, then you can tie them up before they start to flop. This will also help you to remember where you planted them.

“I have always planted lilies in spring, but an online site is offering them for sale now. Will they be all right if I plant them in autumn?”

As long as the soil or compost is free-draining and not likely to waterlog at any time during winter, they should be perfectly safe.

“Which bulbs can I plant in autumn for cut flowers next spring?”

Grape hyacinths (*Muscari*), narcissi, tulips, Dutch irises and star of Bethlehem (*Ornithogalum umbellatum*) bulbs are planted in autumn and make wonderful cut flowers.

“Last year, I planted some *Iris reticulata* in the rockery. Will they flower again next year or should I plant some more?”

After flowering, *Iris reticulata* bulbs often split into many small offsets. These may take a year or two to reach flowering size again, so if you want to see the flowers in your rock garden next year, you should plant some more.

"IS THERE ANY WAY I CAN MAKE SURE THAT DRY SNOWDROP BULBS WILL FLOWER NEXT YEAR?"

Some of them will take a year or two to come back into flower whatever you do, but if you buy and plant them as soon as they are offered for sale, they stand a better chance of flowering.

"I PLANT TUBERS OF WINTER ACONITES (*ERANTHIS*) EVERY AUTUMN, BUT NEVER SEEM TO GET A GOOD SHOW. WHAT AM I DOING WRONG?"

These are often better grown in pots and planted out when they are in full flower and leaf in spring. They seed readily after flowering, so never hoe round them once the flowers have faded.

"When should I plant *Anemone coronaria* tubers?"

Plant them in autumn for flowering in spring, or in spring for flowering in summer and early autumn.

"My flat has a tiny, sunny balcony. Can you suggest some plants for winter interest?"

Winter heathers and dwarf conifers will give a good display and last for many years, and winter-flowering pansies bloom from autumn until early summer.

"WHAT BULBS SHOULD I BE PLANTING IN MY CONTAINERS FOR SPRING FLOWERING?"

Crocuses, dwarf daffodils and botanical tulips will give you 'a bright splash' from late winter and throughout the spring.

“Is it possible to have a semi-permanently planted winter hanging basket?”

Yes. Use the largest solid-sided basket you can find, and fill it with soil-less compost. Suitable plants are winter heathers, primulas and polyanthus, dwarf thymes and other evergreen herbs, and periwinkle. Do not overplant, and add new pansies and forget-me-nots every autumn. A basket like this should last about three years.

"Last year I planted daffodils in hanging baskets and they looked untidy. What can I do with the bulbs?"

Taller narcissi tend to fall over in hanging baskets, so replant the bulbs in a large container or tub.

"I WANT TO PLANT SOME BULBS IN CONTAINERS. HOW CAN I GET THE BEST POSSIBLE SHOW?"

Plant in layers, starting with the largest bulbs (standard narcissi and tulips) first, and ending with the small bulbs, like snowdrops (*Galanthus*). This will give you flowers in a single container from midwinter to late spring, longer if you add some alliums.

"WILL BULBS IN CONTAINERS FLOWER THE SECOND YEAR?"

If you use a soil-based potting compost and keep them well fed and watered until the foliage dies, they will come up and flower for several years.

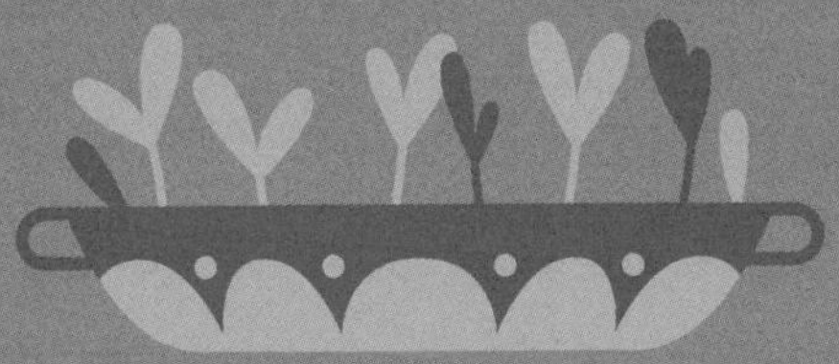

"When I'm replacing summer bedding with winter and spring plants, can I use the same compost?"

You will find that the top layer will be full of roots and much of it will come up with the discarded bedding, so it is better to start again. If you have deep pots, however, replacing the top half with new compost is usually adequate.

"LAST WINTER, THE COMPOST IN MY OUTDOOR POTS GOT SOGGY AND MANY PLANTS DIED. SHOULD I ADD SOMETHING TO THE SOIL TO PREVENT THIS?"

No. Improve the drainage in autumn by checking that the holes in the container bases are not blocked. Use pot feet or bricks to raise the containers off the ground.

"CAN I PLANT PANSIES ON TOP OF SPRING BULBS IN A CONTAINER?"

It depends on the bulbs. Crocuses will work well, but bulbs with large leaves will smother the pansies.

"I have some wire hanging baskets. Should I plant the sides as well when I'm planting them up in autumn?"

Wire hanging baskets are not the best for autumn planting because they freeze more quickly and the plants in the sides often get damaged by strong winds. Invest in some solid-sided ones for overwintering outdoors, or keep the baskets in a cold greenhouse until early spring.

"I HAVE A WINDOW BOX CONTAINING A 'NEW WAVE' TRAILING PETUNIA THAT SURVIVED OUTDOORS ALL LAST WINTER AND HAS BEEN MAGNIFICENT THIS SUMMER. IS THIS UNUSUAL?"

Although we treat them as annuals, petunias are really perennials. The window box will be getting some heat through the window, and the house wall is warmer than the open garden. Out of interest, see if it survives another winter.

"The bottom of my garden is boggy. What can I plant there?"

An easy and inexpensive approach would be to have a bog garden. Plants like candelabra primulas, marsh marigold (*Caltha*), rodgersia, *Lobelia cardinalis* and arum lilies would love these conditions, and provide interest from spring to autumn.

"How can I quickly cover a large fence?"

Try *Lonicera japonica* 'Halliana', a fast-growing, fragrant honeysuckle that can be cut back fairly hard once it has covered the fence.

"WHAT FLOWERING PLANTS CAN I GROW IN SHADE UNDER CONIFERS?"

No flowering plants grow well in this situation. Instead, use tubs of bedding plants and plant some spare ones to replace the originals when necessary. They will soon revive in a sunny spot and can be reused.

"I DON'T SEEM TO HAVE MUCH LUCK WITH MAGNOLIAS. IS THERE AN EASY ONE?"

Magnolia 'Susan' will tolerate most soils. It makes a small tree quite quickly and flowers from an early age.

"I would like a *Buddleja davidii* to attract butterflies. Don't these shrubs get too large for small gardens?"

The cultivars 'Nanho Blue' and 'Nanho Purple' seldom grow more than 1.2 m (4 ft) tall if they are pruned hard each spring.

"I HAVE JUST BOUGHT A GARDENIA. WHERE SHOULD I KEEP IT OVER WINTER?"

A heated conservatory or light windowsill indoors is best.

"ARE THERE ANY BEDDING PLANTS I CAN SOW IN AUTUMN IN THE GREENHOUSE?"

You can sow pansies and sweet peas (*Lathyrus odoratus*) at this time of year.

"When I put my spring bedding plants in, I am left with a lot of perfectly good summer bedding plants, such as *Begonia semperflorens* and coleus (*Solenostemon*). What I can do with these, apart from consigning them to the compost heap?"

Many summer bedding plants can be potted up at the end of the season and taken into the conservatory or greenhouse, or even put on a light windowsill indoors. They will then continue to give pleasure for several more weeks.

"My camellia is getting too large and heavy to move into my greenhouse in autumn. Can I leave it outdoors?"

As long as it is in a position where the flowers will not get early sun in spring, it will be quite safe outdoors.

WINTER

"Why do my Christmas roses (*Helleborus niger*) always flower at different times?"

Some strains come into flower earlier than others, and much depends on the temperature. Most will flower at some time from late winter through spring, and covering them with a cloche will encourage them to flower earlier.

"Is there a tree that will be in flower for a Northern-hemisphere Christmas?"

The winter-flowering cherry (*Prunus × subhirtella* 'Autumnalis') should be in flower, unless the winter is very cold.

“How and when can I prune back an overgrown white rose trained over an arch?”

In winter, remove all dead, dying and weak wood. Cut back some older shoots hard in order to encourage new growth, and trim the shoots that have borne flowers to about 10 cm (4 in) from the base.

“I took some branches off my flowering cherry in early winter, and now I learn I should have done the job in summer. Have I killed the tree?”

Possibly not. Paint the cuts with a fungicidal pruning compound and keep your fingers crossed.

"When should I prune an overgrown *Mahonia japonica*?"

Prune immediately after flowering, which is generally in late winter.

"HOW SHOULD I PRUNE A WINTER JASMINE (*JASMINUM NUDIFLORUM*)?"

After flowering, prune back all the flowered shoots to the main branch framework.

"WHEN I'M PRUNING ROSES AND SIMILAR PLANTS, SHOULD THE CUT SLOPE TOWARDS OR AWAY FROM THE BUD?"

The cut should slope downwards, away from the bud, so that water will drain off and not rot the bud.

"IS IT TRUE THAT YOU SHOULDN'T REMOVE THE OLD HEADS OF HYDRANGEA BUSHES UNTIL AFTER THE RISK OF FROST HAS PASSED?"

This used to be recommended because the dead heads protected the new, flowering shoots underneath from frost. As we now seem to be experiencing warmer winters though, it is unlikely the new growth will be damaged if you want to tidy the plants earlier.

"I put my garden compost on the roses every winter. Why do they never look particularly healthy?"

You need a large amount of compost or manure to give most plants all the nutrients they need and supplementary feeding during the growing season with blood, fish and bone, a balanced fertilizer or a specific plant fertilizer is nearly always necessary.

“What ornamental plants can I grow in my unheated greenhouse in winter?”

Hardy annuals in pots will give you early-spring interest. Many ferns can be displayed under glass in winter, then moved outdoors in summer. Indoor cyclamen will flower if the greenhouse is insulated.

“When should I start cutting back overwintering fuchsias, *Plectranthus* and pelargoniums in my cool greenhouse?”

As soon as you see new leaves, you can prune these plants back hard and repot them.

“HOW CAN I KEEP A STANDARD FUCHSIA ALIVE IN MY UNHEATED GREENHOUSE?”

Wrap the vulnerable stem in pipe lagging over winter.

"WHEN CAN I TAKE CUTTINGS OF MY TENDER FUCHSIAS?"

Take these as soon as shoots appear that are long enough to use as cuttings, usually from late winter on.

"HOW DO I TAKE CHRYSANTHEMUM CUTTINGS IN THE GREENHOUSE?"

In midwinter, take cuttings about 8 cm (3 in) long of basal growths (not side-shoots).

"Why did my seed-grown pelargoniums not flower until late summer last year?"

You probably sowed rather late. Sow in a heated propagator in winter and prick out when large enough, and at a temperature of no less than 13–15°C (55–59°F).

“How do I keep my tender fuchsias over winter without a greenhouse?”

Dig a trench in the garden and bury them. Remember to mark the trench so that you know where they are.

“Is it possible to keep pelargoniums from year to year without a greenhouse?”

Shake off some soil or compost and pack them into boxes. Keep them in a frost-free place, such as a garage.

“IS IT TRUE YOU CAN SAVE PELARGONIUMS BY HANGING THEM UPSIDE DOWN?”

Hang them upside down in a frost-free place, with a little soil or compost still on the roots, and you may save up to 90 per cent of them.

"How can I stop my pulmonarias looking so lack-lustre after flowering?"

Remove the old flower stalks after seeding and cut off the old leaves. The plants will soon produce new, well-marked foliage.

"CAN I CUT BACK MY LEGGY PENSTEMONS?"

Wait until you see new growth coming from low down on the stems in late winter or early spring, then cut back to 5–8 cm (2–3 in) from the base.

"When should I cut back my hellebores?"

Wait until they have seeded, because you will get many seedlings that can be used elsewhere in the garden, then remove all old leaves and flower stalks.

"How can I stop my dahlia tubers from rotting?"

Remove the rotten ones immediately and check the rest for soundness. Dahlia tubers should always be stored upside down so that the remaining sap can drain out. Dust with fungicide.

"Is it necessary to take up half-hardy plants, such as dahlias and gladioli, for the winter?"

In warmer areas, half-hardy plants might overwinter successfully in the ground if you cover them with a mulch of straw or compost. Remove this in spring.

"CAN I HAVE HALF-HARDY PATIO PLANTS OUTDOORS IN WINTER WITHOUT ILL EFFECT?"

Tender fuchsias, pelargoniums, marguerites and osteospermums may be quite happy outdoors in winter in mild areas. However, if you value them, it is best to give them some protection.

"I pruned my roses in autumn and they now have shoots on them. What should I do to prevent frost damage?"

Rose shoots produced in colder weather are much hardier than those appearing after spring pruning. It is unlikely, therefore, that frost will do any serious damage.

"What should I do with bulbs that have flowered indoors?"

After flowering, move them to a cool, light place and feed and water until the leaves start to yellow. Then plant them in the garden. You can either do this straight away or dry them off for autumn planting.

"DO I PLANT BULBS THAT HAVE FLOWERED INDOORS AT THE SAME DEPTH AS IN THE POTS?"

No. They should be planted at the depth they would have been if they had been planted outdoors in the first place: that is, three times as deep as the height of the bulb.

"Are there any indoor flowering bulbs I cannot plant outside afterwards?"

Tender narcissi, like *N. papyraceus* ('Paper White') and 'Grand Soleil d'Or', would not survive the frost. 'Prepared' hyacinths may never produce flowers as big outside.